THE EMOTIONS
OUTLINE OF A THEORY

THE EMOTIONS
OUTLINE OF A THEORY

BY

JEAN-PAUL SARTRE

AUTHOR OF "EXISTENTIALISM," ETC.

THE WISDOM LIBRARY

A Division of

THE PHILOSOPHICAL LIBRARY
New York

Distributed to the Trade by
BOOK SALES, INC.
352 Park Avenue South
New York 10, N.Y.
PRINTED IN THE UNITED STATES OF AMERICA

TRANSLATED FROM THE FRENCH
BY BERNARD FRECHTMAN

CONTENTS

THE EMOTIONS
OUTLINE OF A THEORY

INTRODUCTION

PSYCHOLOGY, PHENOMENOLOGY, AND PHENOMENOLOGICAL PSYCHOLOGY

PSYCHOLOGY is a discipline which aspires to be positive; that is, it tries to draw its resources exclusively from experience. The age of associationists is certainly gone, and contemporary psychologists are no longer prohibited from *asking* and *interpreting*. But like the doctor they want to face their object. When one speaks of contemporary psychology it is still necessary to limit the concept of experience, for, in effect, there can be a host of diverse experiences; for example, one may have to decide whether or not there is an experience of essences or values or a religious experience. The psychologist intends to use only two types of well defined experiences, that which gives us the spatial-temporal perception of organized bodies, and the intuitive knowledge of ourselves that is called reflexive experience. If there are any disputes among the psychologists as to method, they can bear almost solely on the following problem: are these two types of information complementary, should one be subordinated to the other, or should one of them be boldly discarded? But they are in agreement on one essential principle: the inquiry should start, before everything else, with *facts*.

If we ask ourselves what a fact is, we see that it is defined by that which one should *meet* in the course of an investigation and that it always presents itself as an unexpected enrichment and a novelty in relation to anterior facts. It is therefore not necessary to count on the facts to organize themselves in a synthetic totality which by itself might yield its meaning. In other words, if one calls anthropology a discipline which claims to define the essence of man and the human condition, psychology—even the psychology of man—is not and never will be anthropology. It does not intend to define and limit *a priori* the object of its inquiry. The idea of man which it accepts is quite empirical: throughout the world are a number of creatures who present analogous natures to experience. Moreover, other sciences, sociology and psychology, proceed to inform us that there are certain objective connections between these creatures.

No more is needed for the psychologist, in the name of a working hypothesis, to accept prudently to limit his investigations provisionally to this group of creatures. The available sources about them are indeed more easily accessible since they live in society, speak a language, and leave traces of their activity. But the psychologist does not commit himself; he does not know whether the notion of man may not be arbitrary. It may be *too vast*; we do not have to put the Australian primitive into the same psychological class as the American workman of 1939. It may be *too narrow*; nothing says that an abyss separates the higher apes from the human being. In any case, the psychologist rigorously guards against considering the men about him as *his fellow-creatures*. This notion of similitude, on the basis of which one might be able to build an anthropology, seems to him ridiculous and dangerous. He will readily admit, with the reservations made above, that he is a man, that is, that he is a part of the class which has been isolated provisionally. But he will take into consideration that this human character should be conferred upon him *a posteriori* and that he can not, insofar as he is a member of that class, be a privileged object of study, except for the sake of experiments. He will therefore learn *from others* that he is man and his nature as a man will not be revealed to him in a particular way by the pretext that he *is* himself what he studies. Like "objective" experimentation, introspection will furnish only facts.

If it is necessary that there be later a rigorous concept of *man*—and even that is doubtful—this concept can be envisaged only as the crown of a finished science, that is, one which is done with forever. It would be still only a unifying hypothesis, invented to co-ordinate and grade the infinite collection of facts which have been brought to light. This is to say that the idea of man, if ever it takes on a positive meaning, will be only a conjecture aiming to establish connections between disparate materials and will attain verisimilitude only by its success. Pierce defined hypothesis as the sum of the experimental results which it allows us to foresee. Thus, the idea of man can be only the sum of the established facts which it allows us to unite. However, if some psychologists were to use a certain conception of man *before* this ultimate synthesis were possible, it would be a strictly personal act, a conducting wire as it were or, better, like an idea in the Kantian sense, and their first duty would be never to lose sight of the fact that it was a regulating concept.

It follows from so many precautions that psychology, insofar as it claims to be a science, can furnish only a sum of miscellaneous facts, most of which have no connection with the others. What can be more different, for example, than the study of the stroboscopic illusion and the inferiority complex? This confusion is not due to chance but to the very principles of the science of psychology. To expect the *fact* is, by definition, to expect the isolated, to prefer, because of positivism, the accidental to the essential, the contingent to the necessary, disorder to order; it is, on principle, to cast what is essential into the future: "That will do for later, when we shall have assembled enough facts." In short, psychologists do not realize that it is just as impossible to get to essence by accumulating accidents as to reach 1 by adding figures to the right of 0.99.

If their only aim is to accumulate details of knowledge there is nothing to be said; one simply does not see what interest there is in these labors of a collector. But if they are animated, in their modesty, by the hope, in itself praiseworthy, that later on, on the basis of their monographs, an anthropological synthesis will be realized, they are in full contradiction with themselves. It will be said that this is precisely the method and ambition of the natural sciences. The answer to that is that the natural sciences do not aim at knowing *the world*, but the possible conditions of certain general phenomena. This notion of *world* has long since vanished beneath the criticism of methodologists, and precisely because one could not both apply the methods of the positive sciences and hope that they would one day lead to discovering the meaning of the synthetic totality which one calls *world*. But *man* is a being of the same type as *the world*. It is even possible as Heidegger believes, that the notions of world and of "human reality" (*Dasein*) are inseparable. Psychology should resign itself to doing without human reality for precisely that reason, supposing at least that this human reality does exist.

Applied to a particular example the study of the emotions, for example, what will the principles and the methods of the psychologist give us? First of all, our knowledge of the emotion will be added *from without* to other knowledge about the physical being. The emotion will present itself as an irreducible novelty in relation to the phenomena of attention, memory, perception, etc. You can, indeed, inspect these phenomena and the empirical notion of them we build following the psychologists; you can turn them about again and again as you please and you will not discover the slightest essential connection with emotion. All the same, the psychologist grants that man has emotions because experience teaches him so.

Thus, emotion is first of all and in principle an *accident*. In textbooks of psychology it is a chapter which follows other chapters, as calcium follows hydrogen or sulphur in textbooks of chemistry. As for studying the possible conditions of an emotion, that is, wondering whether the very structure of human reality makes emotions possible and *how* it makes them possible, that would appear useless and absurd to a psychologist: what good is it to ask whether emotion is possible precisely because it is.

The psychologist will likewise turn to experience

to establish the limits and definition of emotive phenomena. In fact, he would be able to observe there that he already has an *idea* of emotion, since, after inspecting the facts, he will draw a line of demarcation between the facts of emotion and those which are not such; indeed, how could experience furnish him with a principle of demarcation if he did not already have it? But the psychologist prefers to hold to the belief that the facts group themselves before his eyes by themselves. At present it is a matter of *studying* the emotions one has just isolated. To do that we shall agree to realize affecting situations or to turn to those particularly emotive subjects which pathology offers us. We shall then apply ourselves to determining the factors of this complex state; we shall isolate the *bodily reactions* (which, moreover, we shall be able to establish with the greatest precision), the *behavior*, and the *state of consciousness*, properly so called. Following this we shall be able to formulate our laws and offer our explanations; that is, we shall try to unite these three types of factors in an irreversible order. If I am a partisan of the intellectualist theory, for example, I shall set up a constant and irreversible succession between the inner state considered as antecedent and the physiological disturbances considered as consequents.

If, on the contrary, I think with the partisans of the peripheric theory that "a mother is sad because she weeps," I shall, at bottom, limit myself to reversing the order of the factors. In any case, what is certain is that I shall not seek the explanation or the laws of emotion in the general and essential structures of human reality, but *in the processes of the emotion itself*, with the result that even when it has been duly described and explained it will never be anything but one fact among others, a fact closed in on itself which will never permit either of understanding a thing other than itself or of grasping by means of it the essential reality of man.

It was in reaction against the inadequacies of psychology and psychologism that about thirty years ago a new discipline was constituted called phenomenology. Its founder, Husserl, was struck by this truth: essences and facts are incommensurable, and one who begins his inquiry with facts will never arrive at essences. If I seek the psychic facts which are at the basis of the arithmetic attitude of the man who counts and calculates, I shall never arrive at the reconstitution of the arithmetic essences of unity, number, and operation. However, without giving up the idea of experience (the principle of phenomenology is to go to "things themselves" and the basis of these methods is eidetic intuition), it must be made flexible and must take into account the experience of essences and values; it must even recognize that essences alone permit us to classify and inspect the facts.

If we did not have implicit recourse to the essence of emotion, it would be impossible for us to distinguish the particular group of facts of emotivity among the mass of psychic facts. Since one has had implicit recourse to the essence of emotion as well, phenomenology will therefore prescribe that we have explicit recourse to it and, by concepts, that we set up the content of this essence once and for all. One understands well enough that the idea of man can no longer be an empirical concept, the product of historical generalizations, but that, on the contrary, we have to use, without mentioning it, the *"a priori"* essence of *human being* in order to give a somwhat solid basis to the generalizations of the psychologist. But besides, psychology, considered as a science of certain human facts, could not be a beginning because the psychic facts we meet are never the first ones. They are, in their essential structure, man's reactions against the world. Therefore, they assume man and the world and can only take on their true meaning if one has first elucidated these two notions. If we wish to found a psychology, we shall have to go beyond the psychic, beyond man's situation in the world, to the very source of man, the world, and the psychic: the transcendental and the consecutive consciousness which we attain by "phenomenological reduction" or "putting the world in parentheses."

It is this consciousness which must be interrogated, and what gives value to its responses is precisely that it is *mine*. Thus Husserl knows how to take advantage of this absolute proximity of consciousness in relation to itself from which the psychologist had not wished to profit. He takes advantage knowingly and with full security, since every consciousness exists to the exact extent to which it is conscious of existing. But there, as above, he refuses to interrogate consciousness about *facts*; on the transcendental level we should again find the confusion of psychology. What he is going to try to describe and fix by concepts is precisely the essences which preside as the transcendental field unrolls.

Therefore, there will be, for example, a phenomenology of emotion which, after having "put the world in parentheses" will study emotion as a pure transcendental phenomenon—and will do so not by turning to particular emotions but by seeking to attain and elucidate the transcendental essence of emotion as an organized type of consciousness.

Heidegger, another phenomenologist, likewise took as his point of departure this absolute proximity of the investigator and the thing investigated. The thing which differentiates every inquiry about man from other types of rigorous questions is precisely the privileged fact that human reality is *ourselves*. "The existant which we must analyze," writes Heidegger, "is our self. The being of this existant is *mine*." [1] Now it is not a matter of indifference that this human reality is *I* precisely because, for human reality, to exist is always to *assume* its being, that is, to be responsible for it instead of receiving it from the outside like a stone. "And as 'human reality' is essentially its own possibility, this existant can 'choose' itself in its being; it can win itself and can lose itself." [2] This "assumption" of

[1] *Sein und Zeit*, p. 41.
[2] *Ibid.*, p. 41.

24

self which characterizes human reality implies an understanding of human reality itself, however obscure this understanding may be. "In the being of this existant, the latter relates itself to its being."[3] In effect, understanding is not a quality coming to human reality from the outside; it is its characteristic way of existing. Thus, the human reality which is *I* assumes its own being by understanding it. This understanding is mine. I am, therefore, first, a being who more or less obscurely understands his reality as man, which signifies that I make myself man in understanding myself as such. I may therefore interrogate myself and on the basis of this interrogation lead an analysis of the "human reality" to a successful conclusion which can be used as a foundation for an anthropology. Here, of course, it is no longer a question of introspection, first because introspection meets only the fact, then because my understanding of human reality is obscure and not authentic. It must be cleared up and explained.

In any case, the hermeneutic of existence will be able to found an anthropology, and that anthropology will serve as a basis for any psychology. We are, therefore, in a situation which is the reverse of

[3] *Ibid.*, p. 43.

that of the psychologists, since we *start* from the synthetic totality that is man and establish the essence of man *before* making a start in psychology.

At any rate, phenomenology is the study of phenomena—not facts. And by phenomenon must be understood "that which manifests itself," that whose reality is precisely appearance. "And this 'self-manifestation' is not any sort of manifestation . . . the being of the existant is not something 'behind which' there is still something 'which does not appear.' "[4] In effect, for human reality, to *exist* is, according to Heidegger, to assume its own being in an existential mode of understanding; for consciousness, to *exist* is to *appear*, in Husserl's sense of the word. Since appearance is here the absolute, it is appearance which must be described and interrogated. From this point of view, Heidegger thinks that in every human attitude—for example in emotion, since we were speaking of it a little while ago—we shall find the whole of human reality, since emotion is the human reality which assumes itself and which, "aroused," "directs" itself toward the world. As for Husserl, he thinks that a

[4] *Sein und Zeit,* pp. 35–36.

phenomenological description of emotion will bring to light the essential structure of consciousness, since an emotion is precisely a consciousness. And conversely, a problem arises which the psychologist does not even suspect; can types of consciousness be conceived which would not include emotion among their possibilities, or must we see in it an indispensable structure of consciousness? Therefore, the phenomenologist will interrogate emotion *about consciousness* or *about man.* He will ask it not only what it is but what it has to teach us about a being, one of whose characteristics is exactly that he is capable of being moved. And inversely he will interrogate consciousness, human reality, about emotion: what must a consciousness be for emotion to be possible, perhaps even to be necessary?

We can understand, at the present time, the reasons for the psychologist's mistrust of phenomenology. The psychologist's first precaution consists, in effect, of considering the psychic state in such a way that it removes from it all *signification.* The psychic state is for him always a *fact* and, as such, always accidental. And this accidental character is just what the psychologist holds to most. If one should ask a scientist, "Why do bodies attract each other in accordance with Newton's Law?" he will reply, "I know nothing about that; because it happens to be so." And if one should ask him, "What does this attraction *signify*?" he will reply, "It signifies nothing. It is." In like manner, the psychologist, when questioned about emotion, is quite proud of answering, "It is. Why? I know nothing about that. I simply state it. I know nothing about its signification." For the phenomenologist, on the contrary, every human fact is, in essence, significative. If you remove its signification, you remove its nature as human fact. The task of a phenomenologist, therefore, will be to study the signification of emotion. What are we to understand by that?

To signify is to indicate another thing; and to indicate it in such a way that in developing the signification one will find precisely the thing signified. For the psychologist emotion signifies nothing because he studies it as a fact, that is, by cutting it away from everything else. Therefore, it will be non-significative from its beginning; but if every human fact is really significative, the emotion studied by the psychologist is, by its nature, dead, non-psychic, inhuman. If, in the manner of the phenomenologist, we wish to make of emotion a true phenomenon of consciousness, it will, on the contrary, be necessary to consider it as significative from the first. That is, we shall affirm that it *is* strictly to the extent that it signifies. We shall not first lose ourselves in the study of physiological facts, precisely because, taken by themselves and in isolation, they signify *almost* nothing. They are— that's all. But on the contrary, we shall try, by developing the signification of behavior and of the affected consciousness, to make explicit the thing which is signified. We know what the thing signified is from its origin: the emotion signifies, *in its own way*, the whole of consciousness or, if we put ourselves on the existential level, of human reality. It is not an accident because human reality is not an accumulation of facts. It expresses from a definite point of view the human synthetic totality in its entirety. And we need not understand by that that it is the *effect* of human reality. It is the human reality itself in the form of "emotion." That being so, it is impossible to consider emotion as a psychophysiological disorder. It has its essence, its particular structures, its laws of appe   ıg, and its signification. It cannot come to human reality *from the outside*. On the contrary, it is man who *as sumes* his emotion, and consequently emotion is an organized form of human existence.

We have no intention of entering here upon a phenomenological study of emotion. Such a study, if one had to sum it up very briefly, would deal with affectivity as an existential mode of human reality. But our ambitions are more limited. We should like to see a study of emotion in a precise and concrete case, if pure psychology can reasonably extract a method and some lessons from phenomenology. We agree that psychology does not put man into question or the world in parentheses. It takes man in the world as he presents himself through a multitude of situations, in the café, with his family, at war. Generally speaking, what interests it is *man in situations*. As such, it is, as we have seen, subordinate to phenomenology, since a really positive study of man in situations should first have elucidated the notions of man, world, being-in-the-world, and situation. But, after all, phenomenology has scarcely been born and all these notions are quite far from their definitive elucidation. Should psychology wait until phenomenology reaches maturity? We do not think so. But if it does not wait for the definitive establishment of an anthropology, it ought not lose sight of the fact that this anthropology is realizable, and that if one day it is realized, the psychological disciplines will have to have their source there. For the time being, it should not aim so much at gathering facts as at interrogating *phenomena*, that is, to put it exactly, psychic events, insofar as they are significations and not insofar as they are pure facts. For example, it will recognize that emotion *does not exist* as a corporeal phenomenon, since a body cannot be affected, for want of power to confer a meaning on its own manifestations. It will immediately seek something beyond vascular or respiratory disturbances, this something being the *feeling* of joy or sadness. But as this feeling is not exactly a quality imposed on joy or sadness from the outside, as it exists only to the extent to which it appears, that is, to which it is "assumed" by the human reality, it is consciousness itself which it will interrogate, since joy is joy only insofar as it appears as such.

And precisely because it seeks not facts but significations, it will abandon the methods of inductive introspection or external empirical observation to seek only to grasp and fix the essence of phenomena. It will, therefore, also proclaim itself an eidetic science. However, through the psychic phenomenon it will not aim at the *thing signified* as such, that is, the human totality. It does not have sufficient means at its disposal to attempt this study. What will interest it solely is the phenomenon *insofar as it is significative*. In the same way I can try to grasp the essence of the "proletariat" through the word "proletariat." In that case, I will be practising sociology. But the linguist studies the word proletariat *insofar as it signifies proletariat* and he will be uneasy about the vicissitudes of the word as a carrier of signification. Such a science is perfectly possible.

What does it lack to be real? To have shown proofs. We have shown that if human reality appears to the psychologist as a collection of miscellaneous data, it is because the psychologist has readily taken a point of view from which its reality had to appear to him as such. But that does not necessarily imply that human reality is anything other than a collection. What we have proved is only that it *can*not appear otherwise to the psychologist. It remains to know whether it can bear a phenomenological investigation at its roots, that is, whether emotion, for example, is truly a significative phenomenon. The following pages should be regarded as an *experiment* in phenomenological psychology. We shall try to place ourselves on the grounds of signification and to treat emotion as a *phenomenon*.

CHAPTER ONE

THE CLASSICAL THEORIES

WE KNOW all the criticisms which have been raised against the peripheric theory of the emotions. How are we to explain the subtle emotions? Passive joy? How can we grant that commonplace organic reactions can account for qualified psychic states? How can modifications which are qualitative (and, thereby, as if uninterrupted in their vegetative functions) correspond to a qualitative series of states which are irreducible among them? For example, the physiological modifications which correspond to anger differ only in intensity from those which correspond to joy (slightly accelerated respiratory rhythm, slight increase in muscular tonicity, extension of bio-chemical changes, arterial tension, etc.), yet anger is not more intense joy; it is something else, at least insofar as it presents itself to consciousness. It would serve no purpose to show that in joy there is an excitation which predisposes one to anger, to cite idiots who pass continually (for example, while rocking on a bench and accelerating their rocking) from joy to anger. The idiot who is angry is not "ultra joyful." Even if he has *passed* from joy to anger (and nothing allows us to assert that a host of psychic events has not intervened), anger is not reducible to joy.

It seems to me what is common to all these objections could be summed up thus: William James distinguishes two groups of phenomena in emotion, a group of physiological phenomena and a group of psychological phenomena which we shall hereafter call the *state* of consciousness. The essence of his thesis is that the state of consciousness called "joy, anger, etc." is nothing other than the consciousness of physiological manifestations—their projection in consciousness if you like. But all the critics of James, examining "emotion," a "state" of consciousness, and the concomitant physiological manifestations, do not *recognize* projection in the former which is the shadow cast by the latter. They find *more*, and—whether or not they are clearly conscious of it—*something else. More:* one can, in imagination, push bodily disorders to the limit, but in vain; it could not be understood why the corresponding consciousness would be a *terrorized* consciousness. Terror is an extremely painful, even unbearable, state, and it is inconceivable that a bodily state perceived for and in itself should appear to consciousness with this frightful character. *Something else:* in effect, even if emotion perceived objectively presents itself as a physiological disorder, insofar as it is a fact it is not at all a disorder or an utter chaos. It has a meaning; it signifies something. And by that we do not mean only that it presents itself as a pure quality; it sets itself up as a certain relationship of our psychic being with the world, and this relationship, or rather our consciousness of it, is not a chaotic connection between the ego and the universe. It is an organized and describable structure.

I do not see that the cortico-thalamic sensitivity, recently invented by the same ones who make these criticisms of James, allows for a satisfactory answer to the question. First, James's peripheric theory had a great advantage; it took into account only physiological disturbances which could be revealed directly or indirectly. The theory of cerebral sensitivity invokes an unverifiable cortical disturbance.

39

Sherrington has made some experiments on dogs, and one can certainly praise his skill as an operator. But these experiments taken by themselves, prove *absolutely nothing*.

From the fact that the *head of a dog* practically isolated from its body still gives signs of emotion, I do not see that one has the right to conclude that the *dog* experiences a complete emotion. Moreover, even supposing that the existence of a cortico-thalamic sensitivity were established, it would again be necessary to ask the previous question: can a physiological disturbance, *whatever it may be*, account for the *organized* character of emotion?

This is what Janet understood quite well, but expressed unfortunately, when he said that James, in his description of emotion lacked the psychic. Janet taking a strictly objective standpoint, wished to record only the external manifestations of emotion. But he thought that, even considering only the organic phenomena which one can describe and reveal from the exterior, these phenomena immediately admit of being classed in two categories, psychic phenomena, or behavior, and physiological phenomena. A theory of emotion which wishes to restore to the psychic its preponderant role should make of emotion a matter of behavior. But Janet, like James, was sensitive, despite everything, to the appearance of disorder which all emotion presents. Therefore, he makes emotion a less well adapted behavior, or, if one prefers, a behavior of disadaptation, a behavior arising from a setback.

When the task is too difficult and we cannot maintain the superior behavior which would be suitable to it, the psychic energy liberated is spent in another way: we maintain an inferior behavior which requires a lesser physiological tension. Let us take, for example, a young girl whose father has just told her that he has pains in his arms and that he is a little afraid of paralysis. She rolls on the floor, a prey to violent emotion, which returns a few days later with the same violence and finally forces her to seek the help of doctors. In the course of the treatment, she confesses that the idea of taking care of her father and leading the austere life of a sick-nurse had suddenly seemed unbearable. The emotion, therefore, represents in this instance a setback-behavior. It is a substitution for "sicknurse-behavior-unable-to-be-endured." Likewise, in his work on *Obsession and Psychasthenia*, Janet cites the cases of several sick people who, having come to him to confess, could not get to the end of their confession and ended by bursting into sobs, sometimes even by having an attack of hysteria. There again, the behavior to be kept up is too difficult. The tears, the hysteria, represent a setback-behavior which is substituted for the first by diversion from its proper course. It is not necessary to insist; examples abound. Who does not remember having bantered with a friend, having remained calm as long as the contest seemed equal, and having become irritated the very moment he found nothing more to answer? Janet can therefore pride himself on having reintegrated the psychic into emotion; the consciousness which we take of emotion—which consciousness, moreover, is here only a secondary phenomenon [1] is no longer the simple correlative of physiological disorder; it is the consciousness of a setback and a setback-behavior. The theory seems fascinating. It is certainly a *psychological* thesis and has a quite mechanistic simplicity. The phenomenon of derivation is nothing more than a change of path for freed nervous energy.

[1] But not an epiphenomenon: consciousness is the behavior of behavior.

And yet, how many obscurities there are in these few notions which seem to be so clear. To consider the matter more closely, it is noticeable that Janet goes beyond James only by using implicitly a finality which his theory explicitly rejects. In effect, what is setback-behavior? Should we mean by that only the automatic substitution for a superior behavior that we cannot maintain? In that case, nervous energy could discharge itself at random and in accordance with the law of least resistance. But then the ensemble of active reactions would be less a setback-behavior than an absence of behavior. There could be a diffuse organic reaction, a disorder, in place of an adapted reaction. But isn't that precisely what James has said? Does not emotion intervene for him precisely at the moment of an abrupt dis-adaptation, and does it not consist essentially of the ensemble of disorders which this dis-adaptation brings about in the organism? Doubtless, Janet puts more emphasis on the *setback* than James does. But what are we to understand by that? If we consider the individual as a system of behavior, and if the derivation occurs automatically, the setback is nothing; it does not exist; there is simply substitution of one behavior by a diffuse ensemble

43

of organic manifestations. For emotion to have the psychic signification of a setback, consciousness must intervene and confer this signification upon it. It must keep the superior behavior as a possibility and must grasp the emotion precisely as a setback *in relation* to this superior behavior. But this would be to give to consciousness a constitutive role which Janet did not want at any price. If one wanted Janet's theory to retain some meaning, he would be led logically to adopt the position of M. Wallon. In an article in the *Revue des Cours et Conférences*, M. Wallon offers the following interpretation: assume a primitive nervous system, a child's. The ensemble of the new born infant's reactions to tickling, pain, etc., would always be governed by this system (shivering, diffuse muscular contractions, accelerations of the cardiac rhythm, etc.) and would then constitute a first organic adaptation, an inherited adaptation, of course. By what follows we would learn about conduct and would realize new set-ups, that is, new systems. But when in a new and difficult situation, we cannot find the adapted behavior which suits him, there would be a return to the primitive nervous system. It is evident that this theory represents the transposition of

Janet's views on the level of pure behaviorism, since, in short, emotional reactions are regarded not as a pure disorder but as a lesser adaptation: the nervous system of the child, the first organized system of defensive reflexes, is disadapted in relation to the needs of the adult, but in itself it is a functional organization, analogous, for example, to the respiratory reflex. But it is also evident that this thesis is differentiated from that of James only by the supposition of an organic unity which would connect all the emotive manifestations. It goes without saying that James would have accepted the existence of such a system without any difficulty, if it had been proved. He would have held this modification of his own theory as of little importance because it was of a strictly physiological order. Therefore, Janet, if we keep to the terms of his thesis, is much nearer to James than he wished to say. He has failed in his attempt to reintroduce the "psychic" into emotion. He has not explained either why there are *various* forms of setback-behavior, why I may react to abrupt aggression by fear *or* anger. Moreover, almost all the examples he cites come back to slightly differentiated emotional upheavals (sobs, hysteria, etc.) which are much closer to what is properly called emotional shock than to qualified emotion.

But it seems that there is in Janet a subjacent theory of emotion—and, furthermore, of conduct in general—which would introduce finality without naming it. In his general discussions of psychasthenia or affectivity he insists, as we have said, on the automatic character of derivation. But in many of his descriptions he lets it be understood that the sick person throws himself into the inferior behavior *in order not* to maintain the superior behavior. Here it is the sick person himself who proclaims himself checked even before having undertaken the struggle, and the emotive behavior comes to *mask* the impossibility of maintaining the adapted behavior. Let us again take the example which we cited earlier: a sick girl comes to Janet; she wants to confide the secret of her turmoil, to describe her obsession minutely. But she is unable to; such social behavior is too hard for her. *Then* she sobs. But does she sob *because* she cannot say anything? Are her sobs vain attempts to act, a diffuse upheaval which represents the decomposition of too difficult behavior? Or does she sob precisely *in order not to say anything?* At first sight, the difference between these two interpretations seems slight; in both hypotheses there is behavior which is impossible to maintain; in both there is substitution for behavior by diffuse manifestations. Janet also passes easily from one to the other; that is what makes his theory ambiguous. But in reality, these two theories are separated by an abyss. The first, in effect, is purely mechanistic and—as we have seen—rather close to the essence of that of James. The second, on the contrary, really brings us something new; it alone really deserves the title of a psychological theory of the emotions; it alone sees emotion as behavior. That is because, if we re-introduce finality here, we can understand that emotional behavior is not a disorder at all. It is an organized system of means aiming at an end. And this system is *called* upon to mask, substitute for, and reject behavior that one cannot or does not want to maintain. By the same token, the explanation of the diversity of emotions becomes easy; they represent a particular subterfuge, a special trick, each one of them being a different means of eluding a difficulty.

But Janet gave us what he could. He was too uncertain, divided as he was between a spontaneous finalism and a fundamental mechanism. We shall not ask him to expound the pure theory of emotion-behavior. One finds a first draught of it in the disciples of Köhler, notably in Lewin [2] and Dembo.[3] Here is what P. Guillaume has written on the subject in his *Psychology of Form*:[4]

"Let us take the simplest example. the subject is asked to reach an object placed on a chair, but without putting his foot outside a circle drawn on the ground. The distances are calculated so that the thing is very difficult or impossible to do directly, but one can resolve the problem by indirect means. . . . Here the force oriented toward the object takes on a clear and concrete meaning. Besides, in these problems there is an obstacle to the direct execution of the act; the obstacle may be material or moral; for example, it may be a rule which one is bound to observe. Thus, in our example, the circle which one must not overstep forms a barrier in the subject's perception from which

[2] Lewin, "Vorsatz, Wille und Bedürfnis," *Psy. Forschung,* VII, 1926.

[3] Dembo, "Der Aerger als dynamisches Problem," *Psy. Forschung,* 1931, pp. 1–144.

[4] Bib. de Philosophie scientifique, pp. 138–142.

there emanates a force directed in an opposite direction to that of the first.

The conflict of the two forces produces a tension in the phenomenal field. . . . When the solution has been found, the successful act puts an end to his tension. There is a whole psychology of the act of replacement or substitution, of ersatz, to which the school of Lewin has made an interesting contribution. Its form is very variable. The half-results attained may help to stabilize it. Sometimes the subject facilitates the act by freeing himself from some of the imposed conditions of quantity, quality, speed, and duration, and even by modifying the nature of his task. In other cases it is a matter of unreal, symbolic acts; one makes an evidently vain gesture in the direction of the act; one describes the act instead of doing it; one imagines fantastic, fictitious procedures (if I had . . . I would have to . . .) outside of the real or imposed conditions which would permit of its being accomplished. If the acts of substitution are impossible or if they do not produce sufficient resolution, the persistent tension manifests itself by the tendency to give up, to run away, or to retire into oneself in an attitude of passivity. We have said, in effect, that the subject finds himself submissive to the positive attraction of the goal, to the negative attraction of the barrier. Moreover, the fact of having agreed to submit to the test has conferred a negative value on all other objects in the field, in this sense, that all diversions foreign to the task are *ipso facto* impossible. The subject is therefore enclosed in some way in a circuit which is closed everywhere: there is only one positive way out, but it is closed by the specific barrier. This situation corresponds to the diagram below:

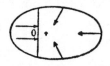

Escape is only a brutal solution since one has to break the general barrier and accept a diminution of the self. Withdrawing into oneself, the *encystment* which raises a protective barrier between the hostile field and the self, is another equally feeble solution.

The continuation of the test can end in conditions of emotional disorder, other still more primitive forms of the freeing of tensions. The attacks of sometimes very violent anger which occur in cer-

tain persons have been well studied in the work of
T. Dembo. The situation undergoes a structural
simplification. In anger, and doubtless in all other
emotions, there is a weakening of the barriers which
separate the deep and the superficial layers of the
self and which normally assure control of actions
by the deep personality and the mastery of the self;
a weakening of the barriers between the real and
unreal. Contrariwise, from the fact that action is
blocked, tensions between the external and the internal continue to increase; the negative character
extends uniformly to all objects in the field which
lose their proper value. . . . The privileged direction of the goal having disappeared, the differentiated structure which the problem has imposed on
the field is destroyed. . . . The particular facts,
notably the varied physiological reactions, to which
some psychologists have attributed a particular
signification, are intelligible only on the basis of
this combined conception of the topology of emotion."

We have now arrived, at the end of this long
quotation, at a functional conception of anger.
Anger is certainly neither an instinct nor a habit
nor a reasoned calculation. It is an abrupt solution

of a conflict, a way of cutting the Gordian Knot. And we certainly come back to Janet's distinction between superior behavior and inferior or derived behavior. Only, this distinction now takes on its full meaning: it is we who put ourselves into a state of complete inferiority, because on this very low level our needs are fewer; we are satisfied, and with less expense. Being unable, in the state of high tension, to find the delicate and precise solution of a problem we act upon ourselves, we lower ourselves, and we transform ourselves into the kind of being who is satisfied with crude and less well adapted solutions (for example, tearing up the paper which gives the statement of the problem). Thus, anger appears here as an escape; the subject in anger resembles a man who, lacking the power to undo the knots of the ropes which bind him, twists and squirms about in his bonds. And the behavior of "anger," less well adapted to the problem than the superior—and impossible—behavior which would resolve it, is, however, precisely and perfectly adapted to the need of breaking the tension, of shaking off that leaden cloak which weighs on our shoulders. Henceforth, one will be able to understand the examples which we cited

earlier: the psychasthenic who went to see Janet
wanted to confess to him. But the task was too difficult. There she was in a narrow and threatening
world which expected her to perform a precise act
and which repulsed her at the same time. Janet
himself indicated by his attitude that he was listen-
ing and waiting. But, at the same time, by his pres-
tige, his personality, and so on, he repelled this
confession. It was necessary to escape this intoler-
able tension, and the sick person could do so only
by exaggerating her weakness and her confusion,
by turning her attention from the act to be done in
order to bring it back to herself ("how unhappy I
am"), by transforming Janet, by her very attitude,
from a judge to a comforter, by externalizing and
enacting her very lack of power to talk, by can-
celing the precise necessity of giving such and such
information about the heavy and undifferentiated
pressure which the world exerted upon her. That
was the moment for the sobs and the hysteria to
appear. Likewise, it is easy to understand the fit of
anger which seized me when I could no longer
reply to someone with whom I had been bantering.
Anger in this case had not quite the same role as
in Dembo's example. It was a matter of carrying

on the discussion on another plane: I was unable
to be witty; I made myself formidable and intimi-
dating. I wanted to inspire fear. At the same time
I used derived (ersätze) means to conquer my
opponent: abuse and threats which were *equiva-
lents for* the witticism I could not find, and, by the
abrupt transformation which I imposed upon myself, I became less exacting in my choice of means.

Yet we cannot be satisfied with the point we
have reached. The theory of behavior-emotion is
perfect, but in its very purity and perfection we
can see its insufficiency. In all the examples we
have cited, the functional role of emotion is un-
deniable. But as such it is also incomprehensible.
I understand that for Dembo and the psychologists
of form the passage from the state of inquiry to the
state of anger is explained by the breaking of one
form and the reconstitution of another. And I
understand the breaking of the form "problem-
without-a-solution" in a very strict sense; but how
can I admit the appearing of the other form? It
must be thought of as being clearly given as the
substitute of the first. It exists only in relation to the
first. Therefore there is a single process, namely,
transformation of form. But I cannot understand

this transformation without first supposing consciousness, which, alone, by its synthetic activity, can break and reconstitute forms ceaselessly. It alone can account for the finality of emotion. Besides, we have seen that the entire description of anger given by Guillaume, following Dembo, shows it to us as aiming to transform the aspect of the world. It is a matter of "weakening the barriers between the real and the unreal" and "destroying the differentiated structure which the problem has imposed upon the field." Splendid; but as soon as it is a question of setting up a connection from the world to the self, we can no longer be content with a psychology of form. We must evidently have recourse to consciousness. And moreover, in the last analysis, isn't that what Guillaume has recourse to when he says that the angry person "weakens the barriers which separate the deep and superficial levels of the self?" Thus, the physiological theory of James has led us by its very inadequacy to Janet's theory of behavior, which, in turn, has led us to the functional theory of emotion-form, and this, in turn, finally, sends us back to consciousness. That is what we should have begun with. It is now time to formulate the real problem.

CHAPTER TWO

THE PSYCHOANALYTIC THEORY

ONE CAN understand emotion only if he looks for a *signification*. This signification is by nature of a functional order. We are therefore led to speak of a finality of emotion. We grasp this finality in a very concrete way by objective examination of emotional behavior. It is not at all a matter of a more or less obscure theory of emotion-instinct based on *a priori* principles or on postulates. The simple consideration of facts leads us to an empirical intuition of the finalist signification of emotion. If, on the other hand, we try to establish the essence of emotion as a fact of interpsychology in a full intuition, we grasp this finality as inherent in its structure. And all psychologists who have reflected on James's peripheric theory have been more or less conscious of this finalist signification. This is what Janet adorns with the name "psychic." It is what psychologists or physiologists like Cannon and Sherrington tried to reintroduce into the description of emotive facts with their hypothesis of a cerebral sensitivity; again, this is what we find in Wallon or, more recently, in the psychologists of form. This finality supposes a synthetic organization of behavior which can be only the unconscious of the psychoanalysts or consciousness. But it would be rather easy, if it were necessary, to have a psychoanalytic theory of emotion-finality. One could, without too much trouble, show anger or fear to be means used by unconscious tendencies to satisfy themselves symbolically or to break a state of unbearable tension. One could account for this essential character of emotion as follows: one *undergoes* it; it takes one by surprise; it develops in accordance with its own laws and without our conscious spontaneity's being able to modify its course appreciably. This dissociation of the organized character of emotion, whose organizing theme one could cast into the unconscious, and of its inevitable character, which would be such only for the consciousness of the subject, would render about the same service on the plane of empirical psychology as the Kantian distinction between empirical character and noumenal character does on the metaphysical plane.

Psychoanalytical psychology has certainly been the first to put the emphasis on the signification of psychic facts; that is, it was the first to insist upon the fact that every state of consciousness is the equivalent of something other than itself. For example, the clumsy theft carried out by a person who is sexually obsessed is not simply a "clumsy theft." As soon as we consider it with the psychoanalysts as a phenomenon of self-punishment it sends us back to something other than itself. It sends us back to the first complex for which the sick person is trying to justify himself by punishing himself. One can see that a psychoanalytic theory of emotion could be possible. Does it not already exist? A woman has a phobia of bay-trees. As soon as she sees a cluster of bay-trees, she faints. The psychoanalyst discovers in her childhood a painful sexual incident connected with a laurel bush. Therefore, what will the emotion be in such a case? A phenomenon of refusal, of censure. Not of refusal *of the bay-tree*. A refusal to re-live the memory connected with the bay-tree. The emotion here is flight from the revelation to be made, as sleep is sometimes a flight from a decision to be made, as the sickness of some young girls is, for Stekel, a flight

from marriage. Of course, emotion will not always
be escape. One can already begin to see among the
psychoanalysts an interpretation of anger as a symbolic gratification of sexual tendencies. And, of
course, none of these interpretations is to be re-
jected. There can be no doubt that anger may
signify sadism. That fainting from passive fear may
signify flight, the search for a refuge, is certain, and
we shall try to show the reason for it. What is in
question here is the very principle of psychoanalytical explanation. That is what we should like to
consider here.

The psychoanalytical interpretation considers
the phenomenon of consciousness as the symbolic
realization of a desire repressed by censorship. Let
us note that for consciousness this desire *is not im-
plicated in its symbolic realization*. Insofar as it
exists by and in our consciousness, it is only what it
appears to be: emotion, desire for sleep, theft,
phobia of bay-trees, etc. If it were otherwise and
if we had some consciousness, *even implicit*, of our
real desire, we should be *dishonest*; the psychoanalyst does not mean it that way. It follows that
the signification of our conscious behavior is entirely
external to the behavior itself, or, if one prefers, the

thing signified is entirely cut off from the *thing signifying*. The behavior of the subject is, in itself, what it is (if we call "in itself" what it is *for itself*), but it is possible to decipher it by appropriate techniques as a written language is deciphered. In short, the conscious fact is to the thing signified as a thing, the *effect* of a certain event, is to that event, for example, as the traces of a fire lit on the mountain are to the human beings who lit the fire. Human presences are not *contained* in the ashes which remain. They are connected with them by a bond of causality; the bond is *external*, the remains of the fire are *passive* in relation to this causal relationship as is every effect in relation to its cause. A consciousness which has not acquired the necessary technical knowledge would be unable to perceive these traces as *signs*. At the same time, these traces are what they are, that is, they exist in themselves outside of any signifying interpretation; they *are* half-calcinated pieces of wood; that is all.

May we admit that a fact of consciousness may be like a thing in relation to its signification, that is, may receive it from without like an external quality —as it is an external quality for the burnt wood to have been burned by men who wanted to warm themselves? It seems, at the start, that the first result of such an interpretation is to establish consciousness as a thing in relation to the thing signified; it is to admit that consciousness is established as a signification without being conscious of the signification which it establishes. There is a flagrant contradiction here, unless one does not consider consciousness as an existence like a stone or a cart. But in this case it is necessary to renounce entirely the Cartesian cogito and make of consciousness a secondary and passive phenomenon. Insofar as consciousness *makes itself*, it is never anything but what it appears to be. Therefore, if it possesses a signification it should contain it in itself as a structure of consciousness. This does not at all mean that this signification has to be perfectly explicit. Many degrees of condensation and clarity are possible. It means only that we should not examine consciousness from without as one examines the traces of the fire or the encampment, but from within, that one should find signification *in it*. If the cogito is to be possible, consciousness is itself the *fact*, the *signification*, and the *thing signified*.

The truth is that what makes an exhaustive refutation of psychoanalysis difficult is that the psychoanalyst does not consider signification as being conferred upon consciousness from without. For him there is always an internal analogy between the conscious fact and the desire which it expresses, since the *conscious fact symbolizes with the complex which is expressed.* And for the psychoanalyst this character of symbol is evidently not external to the fact of consciousness itself; it is constitutive. We are completely in agreement with him on this point: that symbolization is constitutive of symbolic consciousness will trouble no one who believes in the absolute value of the Cartesian cogito. But it must be understood that if symbolization is constitutive of consciousness, it is permissible to perceive that there is an immanent bond of *comprehension* between the symbolization and the symbol. Only, we shall have to agree upon what it is that consciousness *is constituted of* in symbolization. In that case, there is nothing behind it, and the relation between symbol, thing symbolized, and symbolization is an interstructural bond of consciousness. But if we add that consciousness symbolizes under the causal pressure of a transcendant fact which is the repressed desire, we again fall into the previously described theory which makes the relation of thing signified to thing signifying a causal relation. It is the profound contradiction of all psychoanalysis to introduce *both* a bond of causality and a bond of comprehension between the phenomena which it studies. These two types of connection are incompatible. Also, the psychoanalytic theoretician establishes transcendant bonds of rigid causality among the facts studied (in dreams, a pin cushion always *signifies* woman's breasts; entering a railway-carriage *signifies* performing the sexual act), whereas the practitioner is confident of getting successful results by studying, above all, the facts of consciousness in comprehension, that is, by seeking in a flexible way, the intra-conscious relationship between symbolization and symbol.

As for us, we do not reject the results of psycho-analysis when they are obtained by comprehension. We limit ourselves to denying any value and any intelligibility to its subjacent theory of psychic causality. And, moreover, we assert, that to the extent to which the psychoanalyst makes use of *comprehension* to interpret consciousness it would be better freely to recognize that everything which takes place in consciousness can receive its explanation only from consciousness itself. So we have returned to our point of departure: a theory of emotion which insists on the signifying character of emotive facts should seek this signification in consciousness itself. In other words, it is consciousness which *makes itself* consciousness, being moved to do so by the needs of an inner signification.

The fact is that partisans of psychoanalysis will immediately raise a difficulty of principle: if consciousness organizes emotion as a certain type of response adapted to an exterior situation, how does it come about, therefore, that it does not have consciousness of this adaptation? And it must be recognized that their theory accounts perfectly for the wedging between signification and consciousness, which ought not to astonish us since it is made precisely for that purpose. Better still, they will say, in most cases we struggle as a conscious spontaneity against the development of emotional manifestations; we try to master our fear, to calm our anger, to hold back our sobs. Thus, not only do we not have consciousness of the finality of emotion but we still repress emotion with all our strength, and it invades us in spite of ourselves. A phenomenological description of emotion owes it to itself to remove these contradictions.

CHAPTER THREE

A SKETCH OF A PHENOME-NOLOGICAL THEORY

Perhaps what will help us in our investigation is a preliminary observation which may serve as a general criticism of all the theories of emotion which we have encountered (except, perhaps, Dembo's theory). For most psychologists everything takes place as if the consciousness *of* the emotion were first a reflective consciousness, that is, as if the first form of the emotion as a fact of consciousness were to appear to us as a modification of our psychic being or, to use everyday language, to be first perceived as a *state of consciousness*. And certainly it is always possible to take consciousness of emotion as the affective structure of consciousness, to say "I'm angry, I'm afraid, etc." But fear is not originally consciousness *of* being afraid, any more than the perception of this book is consciousness *of* perceiving the book. Emotional consciousness is, at first, unreflective, and on this plane it can be conscious of itself only on the non-positional mode. Emotional consciousness is, at first, consciousness *of* the world. It is not even necessary to bring up the whole theory in order clearly to understand this principle. A few simple observations may suffice, and it is remarkable that the psychologists of emotion have never thought of making them. It is evident, in effect, that the man who is afraid is afraid *of* something. Even if it is a matter of one of those indefinite anxieties which one experiences in the dark, in a sinister and deserted passageway, etc., one is afraid *of* certain aspects of the night, of the world. And doubtless, all psychologists have noted that emotion is set in motion by a perception, a representation-signal, etc. But it seems that for them the emotion then withdraws from the object in order to be absorbed into itself. Not much reflection is needed to understand that, on the contrary, the emotion returns to the object at every moment and is fed there. For example, flight in a state of fear is described as if the object were not, before anything else, a flight *from* a certain object, as if the object fled did not remain constantly present in the flight itself, as its theme, its reason for being, *that from which one flees.* And how can one talk about anger, in which one strikes, injures, and threatens, without mentioning the person who represents the objective unity of these insults, threats, and blows? In short, the affected subject and the affective object are bound in an indissoluble synthesis. Emotion is a certain way of apprehending the world. Dembo is the only one who has perceived this, though he gives no reason for it. The subject who seeks the solution of a practical problem is outside in the world; he perceives the world every moment through his acts. If he fails in his atttempts, if he gets irritated, his very irritation is still a way in which the world appears to him. And, between the action which miscarries and the anger, it is not necessary for the subject to reflect back upon his behavior, to intercalate a reflexive consciousness. There can be a continuous passage from the unreflective consciousness "world-acted" (action) to the unreflective consciousness "world-hateful" (anger). The second is a transformation of the other.

To understand better the meaning of what is to follow, it is necessary that the reader bear in mind the essence of *unreflective behavior.* There is too great a tendency to believe that action is a constant passing from the unreflective to the reflective, from the world to ourself. We perceive the problem (unreflectiveness-consciousness *of* the world); then we perceive ourself as having the problem to solve (reflection); on the basis of this reflection we conceive an action insofar as it ought to be carried on *by us* (reflection), and then we go into the world to carry out the action (unreflective), no longer considering anything but the object acted upon. Then, all new difficulties, all partial checks which might require a restriction of adaptation, again send us to the reflective plane. Hence, a constant going and coming, which is constitutive of action.

Now it is certain that we can reflect on our action. But an operation *on* the universe is carried out most often without the subject's leaving the unreflective plane. For example, at this moment I am writing, but I have no consciousness of writing. Will it be said that habit has made me unconscious of the movements my hand is making as it forms the letters? That would be absurd. Perhaps I have the habit of writing *particular* words in a *particular* order. In a general way, one should distrust explaining things by ascribing them to habit. In reality, the art of writing is not at all unconscious. It is a present structure of my consciousness. Only, it is not conscious *of* itself. To write is to take an active consciousness *of the words* insofar as they are born under my pen. Not of words insofar as they are written *by me*: I intuitively grasp the words insofar as they have this structural quality of issuing *ex nihilo*, and yet of not being creators of themselves, of being passively created. At the very moment that I form one of them, I do not pay attention to each solitary stroke that my hand forms; I am in a special state of waiting, creative waiting; I wait for the word—which I know in advance—to borrow the hand which writes and the strokes which it forms in order that it may realize itself. To be sure, I am not conscious of the words in the same way as when I look over someone's shoulders and read what he is writing. But that does not mean that I am conscious of myself as writing. The essential differences are as follows: first, my intuitive apprehension of what my neighbor is writing is of the type called "probable evidence." I perceive the words which his hand forms well in advance of its having completely formed them. But at the very moment when, on reading "indep . . .," I intuitively perceive "independent," the word "independent" is given as a probable reality (in the manner of the table or the chair). Contrariwise, my intuitive perception of the words I am writing delivers them to me as certain. It is a matter of a somewhat special certainty; it is not certain that the word "certainty" which I am in the act of writing is going to appear (I may be disturbed, may change my mind, etc.), but it is certain that if it appears, it will appear as such. Thus the action constitutes a class of certain objects in a probable world. Let us say, if you will, that insofar as they are real, future objects, they are probable, but insofar as they are potentialities of the world, they are certain. In the second place, the words which my neighbor is writing make no demands; I contemplate them in their order of successive appearance as I would look at a table or a clotheshanger. On the other hand, the words which I write are *exigences*. The very way I perceive them through my creative activity constitutes them as such; they appear as potentialities *having to be realized*. Not having to be realized *by me*. The *I* does not appear here at all. I simply sense the traction which they exert. I feel their exigence objectively. I see them realizing themselves and at the same time demanding to be realized further. I may very well *think* that the words which my neighbor is forming are demanding their realization from him. I do not *feel* this exigence. On the other hand, the exigence of the words which I form is directly present; it has weight and it is felt. They tug at my hand and guide it. But not in the manner of live and active little demons who might actually push and tug at it; they have a passive exigence. As to *my hand*, I am conscious of it in the sense that I see it directly as the instrument by which the words realize themselves. It is an object in the world, but at the same time, it is present and lived. Here I am at the moment hesitating: shall I write "therefore" or "consequently"? That does not at all imply that I stop and think about it. Quite simply, the potentialities "therefore" and "consequently" appear— as potentialities—and come into conflict. We shall try elsewhere to describe in detail the world acted upon. The thing that matters here is to show that action as spontaneous unreflective consciousness constitutes a certain existential level in the world, and that in order to act it is not necessary to be conscious of the self as acting—quite the contrary. In short, unreflective behavior is not unconscious behavior; it is conscious of itself non-thetically, and its way of being thetically conscious of itself is to transcend itself and to seize upon the world as a quality of things. Thus, one can understand all those exigences and tensions of the world which surrounds us. Thus, one can draw up a "hodological" [1] map of our *umwelt*, a map which varies as a function of our acts and needs. Only, in normal and adapted action, the objects "to be realized" appear as having to be realized in certain ways. The means themselves appear as potentialities which demand existence. This apprehension of the means as the only possible way to reach the end (or, if there are n means, as the only n possible means, etc.) can be called a pragmatistic intuition of the determinism of the world. From this point of view, the world around us—what the Germans call *umwelt*—the world of our desires, our needs, and our acts, appears as if it were furrowed with strict and narrow paths which lead to one or the other determined end, that is, to the appearance of a created object.

[1] Lewin's expression.

Naturally, there are decoys and traps scattered around here and there. This world might be compared to the moving plates of the coin-making machines on which the ball-bearings are made to roll; there are paths formed by rows of pins, and often, at the crossings of the paths, holes are pierced through. The ball-bearings must travel across a determined route, taking determined paths and without falling into the holes. This world is *difficult*. This notion of difficulty is not a reflective notion which would imply a relationship to me. It is there, on the world; it is a quality of the world which is given in the perception (exactly like the paths toward the potentialities and the potentialities themselves and the exigences of objects: books having to be read, shoes having to be assembled, etc.) ; it is the noematical correlative of our activity whether undertaken or only conceived.

At present, we can conceive of what an emotion is. It is a transformation of the world. When the paths traced out become too difficult, or when we see no path, we can no longer live in so urgent and difficult a world. All the ways are barred. However, we must act. So we try to change the world, that is, to live as if the connection between things and their

potentialities were not ruled by deterministic processes, but by magic. Let it be clearly understood
that this is not a game; we are driven against a
wall, and we throw ourselves into this new attitude with all the strength we can muster. Let it also
be understood that this attempt is not conscious of
being such, for it would then be the object of a
reflection. Before anything else, it is the seizure of
new connections and new exigences. The seizure
of an object being impossible or giving rise to a
tension which cannot be sustained, consciousness
simply seizes it or tries to seize it otherwise. In itself
there is nothing strange about this change in the
direction of consciousness. We find a thousand examples of similar transformations in activity and
perception. For example, to look for a face con-
cealed in a picture puzzle ("where is the gun?") is
to lead ourselves perceptibly into the picture in a
new way, to behave before the branches, the tele-
graph poles and the image *as* in front of a gun, to
realize the eye movements which we would make
in front of a gun. But we do not grasp these movements as such. An intention which transcends them
and whose hyle they constitute directs itself through
them upon the trees and the poles which are seized

as "possible guns" until suddenly the perception crystallizes and the gun appears. Thus, through a change of intention, as in a change of behavior, we apprehend a new object, or an old object in a new way. There is no need to start by placing ourselves on the reflective plane. The vignette's inscription serves directly as motivation. We seek the gun without leaving the unreflective plane. That is, a potential gun appears—vaguely localized in the image. The change of intention and behavior which characterizes the emotion must be conceived in the same manner. The impossibility of finding a solution to the problem objectively apprehended as a quality of the world serves as motivation for the new unreflective consciousness which now perceives the world otherwise and with a new aspect, and which requires a new behavior—through which this aspect is perceived—and which serves as hyle for the new intention. But the emotive behavior is not on the same plane as the other behaviors; it is not *effective.* Its end is not really to act upon the object as such through the agency of particular means. It seeks by itself to confer upon the object, and without modifying it in its actual structure, another quality, a lesser existence, or a lesser presence (or a greater existence, etc.). In short, in emotion it is the body which, directed by consciousness, changes its relations with the world in order that the world may change its qualities. If emotion is a joke, it is a joke we believe in. A simple example will make this emotive structure clear: I extend my hand to take a bunch of grapes. I can't get it; it's beyond my reach. I shrug my shoulders, I let my hand drop, I mumble, "They're too green," and I move on. All these gestures, these words, this behavior are not seized upon for their own sake. We are dealing with a little comedy which I am playing *under* the bunch of grapes, through which I confer upon the grapes the characteristic of being "too green" which can serve as a substitute for the behavior which I am unable to keep up. At first, they presented themselves as "having to be picked." But this urgent quality very soon becomes unbearable because the potentiality cannot be realized. This unbearable tension becomes, in turn, a motive for foisting upon the grapes the new quality "too green," which will resolve the conflict and eliminate the tension. Only I cannot confer this quality on the grapes chemically. I cannot act upon the bunch in the ordinary ways. So I seize upon this sourness of the too green grapes by acting disgusted. I magically confer upon the grapes the quality I desire. Here the comedy is only half sincere. But let the situation be more urgent, let the incantatory behavior be carried out with seriousness; there we have emotion.

For example, take passive fear. I see a wild animal coming toward me. My legs give way, my heart beats more feebly, I turn pale, I fall and faint. Nothing seems less adapted than this behavior which hands me over defenseless to the danger. And yet it is a behavior of *escape*. Here the fainting is a refuge. Let it not be thought that this is a refuge *for me*, that I am trying to save *myself* in order not to *see* the wild animal *any more*. I did not leave the unreflective level, but, lacking power to avoid the danger by the normal methods and the deterministic links, I denied it. I wanted to annihilate it. The urgency of the danger served as motive for an annihilating intention which demanded magical behavior. And, by virtue of this fact, I did annihilate it as far as was in my power. These are the limits of my magical action upon the world; I can eliminate it as an object of consciousness, but I can do so only by eliminating consciousness [2] itself. Let it not be thought that the physiological behavior of passive fear is pure disorder. It represents the abrupt realization of the bodily conditions which ordinarily accompany the transition from being awake to sleeping.

The flight into active fear is mistakenly considered as rational behavior. Calculation is seen in such behavior—quick calculation, to be sure—the calculation of someone who wants to put the greatest possible distance between himself and danger. But this is to misunderstand such behavior, which would then be only prudence. We do not flee in order to take shelter; we flee for lack of power to annihilate ourselves in the state of fainting. Flight is a fainting which is enacted; it is a magical behavior which consists of denying the dangerous object with our whole body by subverting the vectorial structure of the space we live in by abruptly creating a potential direction on the *other side*. It is a way of forgetting it, of denying it. It is the same way that novices in boxing shut their eyes and throw themselves at their opponent. They want to eliminate the existence of his fists; they refuse to

[2] Or at least by modifying it; fainting is the transition to dream consciousness, that is, "unrealizing."

perceive them and by so doing symbolically eliminate their efficacity. Thus, the true meaning of fear
is apparent; it is a consciousness which, through
magical behavior, aims at denying an object of the
external world, and which will go so far as to annihilate itself in order to annihilate the object with it.

Passive sadness is characterized, as is well known,
by a behavior of oppression; there is muscular resolution, pallor, coldness at the extremities; one turns
toward a corner and remains seated, motionless,
offering the least possible surface to the world.
One prefers the shade to broad daylight, silence to
noise, the solitude of a room to crowds in public
places or the streets. "To be alone with one's sorrow," as they say. That is not the truth at all. It is
a mark of good character to seem to meditate pro-
foundly on one's grief. But the cases in which one
really cherishes his sorrow are rather rare. The
reason is quite otherwise: one of the ordinary conditions of our action having disappeared, the world
requires that we act in it and on it *without that
condition*. Most of the potentialities which throng
it (tasks *to* do, people *to* see, acts of daily life *to*
carry out) have remained the same. Only the
means of realizing them, the ways which cut

through our "hodological space" have changed. For example, if I have learned that I am ruined, I no longer have the same means at my disposal (private auto, etc.) to carry them out. I have to substitute new media for them (to take the bus, etc.) ; that is precisely what I do not want. Sadness aims at eliminating the obligation to seek new ways, to transform the structure of the world by a totally undifferentiated structure. In short, it is a question of making of the world an affectively neutral reality, a system in total affective equilibrium, of discharging the strong affective charge from objects, of reducing them all to affective zero, and, by the same token, of apprehending them as perfectly equivalent and interchangeable. In other words, lacking the power and will to accomplish the acts which we had been planning, we behave in such a way that the universe no longer requires anything of us. To bring that about we can only act upon our self, only "dim the light," and the noematical correlative of this attitude is what we call *Gloom* ; the universe is gloomy, that is, undifferentiated in structure. At the same time, however, we naturally take the cowering position, we "withdraw into ourselves." The noematical correlative of this attitude is *Refuge*. All the universe is gloomy, but precisely because we want to protect ourselves from its frightening and limitless monotony, we constitute any place whatever as a "corner." It is the only differentiation in the total monotony of the world: a stretch of wall, a bit of darkness which hides its gloomy immensity from us.

Active sadness can take many forms. But the one cited by Janet (the psychasthenic who become hysterical because she did not want to confess) can be characterized as a *refusal*. The question is, above all, one of a negative behavior which aims at denying the urgency of certain problems and substituting others. The sick person wanted Janet's feelings to be moved. That means she wanted to replace the attitude of impassive waiting which he adopted by one of affectionate concern. That was what she wanted, and she used her body to bring it about. At the same time, by putting herself into a state which made confession impossible, she cast the act to be performed out of her range. Thus, as long as she was shaken with tears and hiccups, any possibility of talking was removed. Therefore, the potentiality was not eliminated in this case; the confession remained "to be made." But she had withdrawn from the sick person; she could no longer *want* to do it, but only *wish* to do it some day. Thus, the sick person had delivered herself from the painful feeling that the act was *in her power*, that she was free to do it or not. Here the emotional crisis is the abandoning of responsibility. There is magical exaggeration of the difficulties of the world. Thus, the world preserves its differentiated structure, but it appears as unjust and hostile, because it demands *too much* of us, that is, more than it is humanly possible to give it. The emotion of active sadness in this case is therefore a magical comedy of impotence; the sick person resembles servants who, having brought thieves into their master's home, have themselves tied up so that it can be clearly seen that they could not have prevented the theft. Only, here, the sick person is tied up by himself and by a thousand tenuous bonds. Perhaps it will be said that this painful feeling of freedom which he wants to get rid of is necessarily of a reflective nature. But we do not believe it, and all one need do is observe himself to be aware of this: it is the object which is given as having to be created *freely*, the confession which is given as both *having* to and *being able* to be made.

Of course, there are other functions and other forms of active sadness. We shall not insist upon anger, which we have already spoken of at some length and which, of all the emotions, is perhaps the one whose functional role is must evident. But what is to be said about joy? Does it enter into our description? At first sight it does not seem to, since the joyous subject does not have to defend himself against a change which belittles him, against a peril. But at the very beginning, we must first distinguish between joy-feeling, which represents a balance, an adapted state, and joy-emotion. But the latter, if we consider it closely, is characterized by a certain impatience. Let it be understood that we mean by that that the joyous subject behaves rather exactly like a man in a state of impatience. He does not stay in one place, makes a thousand plans which he immediately abandons, etc. In effect, it is because his joy has been aroused by the appearance of the object of his desires. He is informed that he has acquired a considerable sum of money or that he is going to see again someone he loves and whom he has not seen for a long time. But although the object is "imminent," it is not yet there, and it is not yet *his*. A certain amount of time separates him from the object. And even if it is there, even if the longed-for friend appears on the platform of the station, still it is an object which only yields itself little by little, though the pleasure we have in seeing it is going to lose its edge; we shall never get to the point of holding it there before us as our absolute property, of seizing it at one swoop as a totality (nor will we ever, at one swoop, realize our new wealth as an instantaneous totality. It will yield itself through a thousand details and, so to speak, by "abschattungen"). Joy is a magical behavior which tends by incantation to realize the possession of the desired object as instantaneous totality. This behavior is accompanied by the certainty that the possession will be realized sooner or later, but it seeks to anticipate this possession. The divers activities of joy, as well as muscular hypertension and slight vaso-dilatation, are animated and transcended by an intention which aims through them at the world. This seems easy; the object of our desires appears near and easy to possess. Each gesture is a further approbation. To dance and sing for joy represent symbolically approximate behavior, incantations. By means of these the object, which one could really possess only by prudent and, in spite of everything, difficult behavior, is possessed at one swoop—symbolically. Thus it is, for example, that a man who has just been told by a woman that she loves him, can start dancing and singing. By doing this he abandons the prudent and difficult behavior which he would have to practice to deserve this love and make it grow, to realize slowly and through a thousand little details (smiles, little acts of attentiveness, etc.) that he possesses it. He even abandons the woman who, as a living reality, represents precisely the pole of all his delicate behavior. He grants himself a respite; he will practice them later. For the moment, he possesses the object by magic; the dance mimics the possession.

Yet we cannot be satisfied with these few remarks. They have allowed us to appreciate the functional role of emotion, but we still do not know very much about its nature.

We must first note that the few examples we have just cited are far from exhausting the variety of emotions. There can be many other kinds of fear, many other kinds of sadness. We merely state that they all are tantamount to setting up a magical world by using the body as a means of incantation. In each case the problem and the behavior are different. To grasp its significance and its finality it would be necessary to know and analyze each particular situation. Generally speaking, there are not four major types of emotion. There are many more, and it would be useful and fruitful to classify them. For example, if the fear of the timid person is suddenly moved to anger (a change of behavior motivated by a change of situation), this is not an ordinary type of anger; it is *fear* which has been *surpassed*. This does not at all mean that it is in some way reducible to fear. It simply retains the antecedent fear and makes it enter its own structure. It is only when one has been convinced of the functional structure of emotion that he will come to understand the infinite variety of emotional consciousness. On the other hand, it is proper to insist upon a fact of major importance: behavior pure and simple *is not emotion*, and pure and simple consciousness of this behavior is not emotion either. Indeed, if it were so, the finalist character of emotion would appear much more clearly, and on the other hand, consciousness would easily be able to free itself from it. Moreover, there are false emotions which are not behavior. If someone gives me a gift which only half interests me, it is possible that I may make an external show of intense joy, that I may clap my hands, that I may jump, that I may dance. However, all this is a comedy. I shall let myself be drawn into it a little, and it would be inexact to say that I *am not* joyful. However, my joy is not real. I shall drop it, I shall cast it off as soon as my visitor has parted. This is exactly what we shall call a *false* joy, bearing in mind that falseness is not a logical characteristic of certain propositions, but an existential quality. In the same way I can have false fear or false sadness. Nevertheless, these false states are distinguished from those of the actor. The actor mimics joy and sadness, but he *is neither* joyful *nor* sad because this kind of behavior is addressed to a fictitious universe. He mimics behavior, but he is not behaving. In the different cases of false emotion which I have just cited, the behavior is not sustained by anything; it exists by itself and is voluntary. But the situation is real, and we conceive it as demanding this behavior. Also, by means of this behavior we intend magically to invest real objects with certain qualities. But these qualities are false.

That need not mean that they are imaginary or that they must necessarily annihilate themselves later. Their falseness arises out of an essential weakness which *presents itself* as violence. The agreeableness of the object which was just given to me exists as an exigence much more than as a reality; it has a sort of parasitic and tributary reality which I strongly feel. I know that I make it appear upon the object by a kind of fascination; let me cease my incantations and it will immediately disappear.

True emotion is quite otherwise; it is accompanied by belief. The qualities conferred upon objects are taken as true qualities. Exactly what is meant by that? Roughly this: the emotion is undergone. One cannot abandon it at will; it exhausts itself, but we cannot stop it. Besides, the behavior which boils down to itself alone does nothing else than sketch upon the object the emotional quality which we confer upon it. A flight which would simply be a journey would not be enough to establish the object as being horrible. Or rather it would confer upon it the formal quality of *horrible*, but not the matter of this quality. In order for us truly to grasp the horrible, it is not only necessary to mimic it; we must be spell-bound, flooded by our own emotion; the formal frame of the behavior must be filled with something opaque and heavy which serves as matter. We understand in this situation the role of purely physiological phenomena: they represent the *seriousness* of the emotion; they are phenomena of belief. They should certainly not be separated from behavior. At first, they present a certain analogy with it. The hyper-tension of fear or sadness, the vaso-constrictions, the respiratory difficulties, symbolize quite well a behavior which aims at denying the world or discharging it of its affective potential by denying it. It is then impossible to draw exactly a borderline between the pure difficulties and the behavior. They finally enter with the behavior into a total synthetic form and cannot be studied by themselves; to have considered them in isolation is precisely the error of the peripheric theory. And yet they are not reducible to behavior; one can stop himself from fleeing, but not from trembling. I can, by a violent effort, raise myself from my chair, turn my thought from the disaster which is crushing me, and get down to work; my hands will remain icy. Therefore, the emotion must be considered not simply as being enacted; it is not a matter of pure demeanor. It is the demeanor of a body which is in a certain state ·

the state alone would not provoke the demeanor; the demeanor without the state is comedy; but the emotion appears in a highly disturbed body which retains a certain behavior. The disturbance can survive the behavior, but the behavior constitutes the form and signification of the disturbance. On the other hand, without this disturbance, the behavior would be pure signification, an affective scheme. We are really dealing with a synthetic form; *in order to believe* in magical behavior it is necessary to be highly disturbed.

In order to understand clearly the emotional process with consciousness as the point of departure, it is necessary to bear in mind the twofold character of the body, which is, on the one hand, an object in the world and, on the other, something directly *lived* by consciousness. We can then grasp the essential point: emotion is a phenomenon of belief. Consciousness does not limit itself to projecting affective signification upon the world around it. It *lives* the new world which it has just established. It lives it directly; it is interested in it; it endures the qualities which behavior has set up This signifies that when, with all paths blocked, consciousness precipitates itself into the magical world of emotion, it does so by degrading itself; it is a new consciousness facing the new world, and it establishes this new world with the deepest and most inward part of itself, with this point of view on the world present to itself without distance. The consciousness which is roused rather resembles the consciousness which is asleep. The latter, like the former, is thrown into a new world and transforms its body as synthetic totality in such a way that it can live and grasp this new world through it.

In other words, consciousness changes the body, or, if you like, the body—as a point of view on the universe immediately inherent in consciousness—puts itself on the level of behavior. There we have the reason why physiological manifestations are, at bottom, very trivial disturbances; they resemble those of fever, of angina pectoris, of artificial over-excitement, etc. They simply represent the total and commonplace disturbance of the body as such (the behavior alone will decide whether the disturbance will be in "diminution of life" or in "enlarge-ment"). In itself it is nothing; quite simply, it rep-resents an obscuring of the point of view of con-sciousness on things *insofar* as consciousness realizes this obscuring and *lives it spontaneously*. Of course, we mean by this obscuring a synthetic totality and not something piecemeal. But on the other hand, as the body is a thing among things, a scientific analysis will be able to distinguish in the "biological-body" or the "thing-body" troubles localized in such or such an organ.

Thus the origin of emotion is a spontaneous and lived degradation of consciousness in the face of the world. What it cannot endure in one way it tries to grasp in another by going to sleep, by approaching the consciousness of sleep, dream, and hysteria. And the disturbance of the body is nothing other than the lived belief of consciousness, insofar as it is seen from the outside. Only it must be noted:

First, that consciousness does not thetically have consciousness of itself as degrading itself in order to escape the pressure of the world; it has only positional consciousness of the degradation of the world which takes place on the magical level. So it is nonthetically conscious of itself. It is to this extent and this extent only that one can say of an emotion that it is not sincere. There is therefore nothing surprising in the fact that the finality of the emotion is not placed by an act of consciousness at the core of the emotion itself. This finality, however, is not unconscious; it exhausts itself in the constitution of the object.

Second, that consciousness is caught in its own trap. Precisely because it lives the new aspect of the world by *believing* in it, it is caught in its own belief, exactly as in dreaming and in hysteria. Consciousness of the emotion is a captive but we do not necessarily mean thereby that anything whatever external to it might have enchained it. It is its own captive in the sense that it does not dominate this belief, that it strives to live, and it does so precisely because it lives it, because it is absorbed in living it. We need not conceive spontaneity of consciousness as meaning that it might always be free to deny something at the very moment that it posits this something. A spontaneity of this kind would be contradictory. Consciousness, by its very nature, transcends itself; it is therefore impossible for it to withdraw into itself so that it may suppose that it is outside in the object. It *knows* itself only on the world. And the doubt, by its very nature, can only be the constitution of an existential quality of the object, namely, the *dubious*, or a reflective activity of reduction; that is, the essential characteristic of a new consciousness directed upon the positional

99

consciousness. Thus, just as consciousness sees the magical world into which it has cast itself, it tends to perpetuate this world in which it holds itself captive; the emotion tends to perpetuate itself. It is in this sense that one can call it undergone; consciousness becomes concerned about its emotion; it rises in value. The more one flees, the more frightened he is. The magical world is delineated, takes form, and then is compressed against the emotion and clasps it; the emotion does not wish to escape, it can attempt to flee the magical object, but to flee it is to give it a still stronger magical reality. And as for this very character of *captivity* —consciousness does not realize it in itself; it perceives it on objects; the objects are captivating, enchaining; they seize upon consciousness. Freedom has to come from a purifying reflection or a total disappearance of the affecting situation.

However, the emotion, such as it is, would not be so absorbing if it apprehended upon the object *only* the exact counterpart of what it is noetically (for example, a certain man is terrifying *at this time*, in *this* lighting, in such circumstances). What is constitutive of the emotion is that it perceives upon the object something which exceeds it beyond measure.

There is, in effect, a world of emotion. All emotions have this in common, that they make a same world appear, a world which is cruel, terrible, gloomy, joyful, etc., but one in which the relationship of things to consciousness is always and exclusively magical. It is necessary to speak of a world of emotion as one speaks of a world of dreams or of worlds of madness, that is, a world of individual syntheses maintaining connections among themselves and possessing *qualities*. But every quality is conferred upon an object only by a passage to infinity. This grey, for example, represents the unity of an infinity of real and possible abschattungen, some of which are green-grey, green seen in a certain light, black, etc. Similarly, the qualities which emotion confers upon the object and the world it confers upon them *ad aeternum*. Of course, if I abruptly perceive an object as horrible, I am not explicitly affirming that it will remain horrible throughout eternity. But the very affirmation of the horrible as a substantial quality of the object is already in itself a passage to infinity. The horrible is now within the thing, at the heart of the thing; it is its affective texture; it is constitutive of it.

Thus, an overwhelming and definitive quality of

the thing appears to us through the emotion. And that is what exceeds and maintains our emotion. The horrible is not only the present state of the thing; it is threatened for the future; it spreads itself over the whole future and darkens it; it is a revelation of the meaning of the world. "The horrible" means precisely that the horrible is a substantial quality; it means that there is the horrible in the world. Thus in every emotion a host of affective pretensions are directed toward the future to set it up in an emotional light. We live emotively a quality which penetrates us, which we suffer, and which exceeds us on every side; at once, the emotion ceases to be itself; it transcends itself; it is not a trivial episode of our daily life; it is intuition of the absolute.

This is what explains the delicate emotions. Through a behavior which is barely outlined, through a slight fluctuation of our physical state, we apprehend an objective quality of the object. The delicate emotion is not at all apprehensive about a slight unpleasantness, a modified wonder, a superficial disaster. It is an unpleasantness, a wonder, a disaster *dimly seen*, perceived through a veil. It is a diminution, one which gives itself out as such. But the object is there; it is waiting, and perhaps the next day the veil will be thrown aside, and we shall see it in broad daylight. Thus, one may be only very slightly affected by all this, if one means thereby the bodily disturbances or the behavior, and yet, through a slight depression, we may fear that our whole life will be disastrous. The disaster is total—we know it—it is profound; but as far as today is concerned, we catch only an imperfect glimpse of it. In this case, and in many others like it, the emotion ascribes more strength to itself than it really has, since, in spite of everything, we see through it and perceive a profound disaster. Naturally, the delicate emotions differ radically from the weak emotions whose affective grasp of the object is slight. It is the intention which differentiates delicate emotion from weak emotion because the behavior and the somatic state may be identical in both cases. But this intention is, in turn, motivated by the situation.

This theory of emotion does not explain certain abrupt reactions of horror and admiration which appear suddenly. For example, suddenly a grinning face appears flattened against the window pane; I feel invaded by terror. Here, evidently, there is no behavior to take hold of ; it seems that the emotion has no finality at all. Moreover, there is, in a general way, something immediate about the perception of the *horrible* in certain faces or situations, and the perception is not accompanied by flight or fainting. Nor even by impulsions to flight. However, if one reflects upon it, it is a question of phenomena which are very particular but which are susceptible of an explanation which fits in with the idea we have just expounded. We have seen that, in emotion, consciousness is degraded and abruptly transforms the determined world in which we live into a magical world. But there is a reciprocal action : this world itself sometimes reveals itself to consciousness as magical instead of determined, as was expected of it. Indeed, we need not believe that the magical is an ephemeral quality which we impose upon the world as our moods dictate. Here is an existential structure of the world which is magical.

We do not wish to enlarge here upon this subject which we are reserving for treatment elsewhere. Nevertheless we can at present point out that the category "magical" governs the interpsychic relations of men in society and, more precisely, our perception of others. The magical, as Alain says, is "the mind dragging among things," that is, an irrational synthesis of spontaneity and passivity. It is an inert activity, a consciousness rendered passive. But it is precisely in this form that others appear to us, and they do so not because of our position in relation to them, not as the effect of our passions, but out of essential necessity. In effect, consciousness can be a transcendent object only by undergoing the modification of passivity. Thus, the meaning of a face is a matter of consciousness to begin with (and not a sign of consciousness), but an altered, degraded consciousness, which is, precisely, passivity. We shall come back to these remarks later and we hope to show that they obtrude themselves upon the mind. Thus, man is always a wizard to man, and the social world is at first magical. It is not impossible to take a deterministic view of the interpsychological world nor to build rational superstructures upon this magical world. But this time it is they which are ephemeral and without equilibrium; it is they which cave in when the magical aspect of faces, of gestures, and of human situations, is too strong. What happens, then, when the superstructures laboriously built by reason cave

in and man finds himself once again abruptly
plunged into the original magic? It is easy to guess;
consciousness seizes upon the magical as magical;
it forcibly lives it as such. The categories of "sus-
picious," of "alarming," designate the magical insofar as it is lived by consciousness, insofar as it
urges consciousness to live it. The abrupt passage
from a rational apprehension of the world to a perception of the same world as magical, if it is motivated by the object itself and if it is accompanied
by a disagreeable element, is horror; if it is accompanied by an agreeable element it will be wonder
(we cite these two examples; there are, of course,
many other cases). Thus, there are two forms of
emotion, according to whether it is we who constitute the magic of the world to replace a deterministic activity which cannot be realized, or whether
it is the world itself which abruptly reveals itself as
being magical. In horror, for example, we suddenly
perceive the upsetting of the deterministic barriers.
That face which appears at the pane—we do not
first take it as belonging to a man who might open
the door and with a few steps come right up to us.
On the contrary, he is given, passive as he is, as
acting at a distance. He is in immediate connection,

on the other side of the window, with our body; we live and undergo his signification, and it is with our own flesh that we establish it. But at the same time it obtrudes itself; it denies the distance and enters into us. Consciousness, plunged into this magical world, draws the body along with it, insofar as the body is belief. It believes in it. The behavior which gives emotion its meaning is no longer *ours*; it is the expression of the face, the movements of the body of the other person which come to form a synthetic whole with the disturbance of our organism. Thus, we again find the same elements and the same structures as those we described a little while ago. Simply, the first magic and the signification of the emotion come from the world, not from ourself. Of course, magic as a real quality of the world is not strictly limited to the human. It extends to things insofar as they can be given as human (the disturbing interpretation of a landscape; of certain objects of a room which retains the traces of a mysterious visitor) or as they bear the mark of the psychic. Besides, of course, this distinction between the two great types of emotion is not absolutely rigorous; there are often mixtures of the two types and most emotions are not pure. It is in this

way that consciousness, by realizing through spontaneous finality a magical aspect of the world, can
create the opportunity to manifest itself as a real
magical quality. And reciprocally, if the world is
given as magical in one way or another it is possible
for consciousness to specify and complete the constitution of this magic, diffuse it everywhere, or, on
the contrary, gather it up and concentrate it on a
single object.

At any rate, it should be noted that emotion is
not an accidental modification of a subject which
would otherwise be plunged into an unchanged
world. It is easy to see that every emotional apprehension of an object which frightens, irritates, sad-
dens, etc., can be made only on the basis of a total
alteration of the world. In order that an object may
in reality appear *terrible*, it must realize itself as an
immediate and magical presence *face to face* with
consciousness. For example, the face which ap-
peared behind the window ten yards from me
must be lived as immediately present to me in its
menacing. But this is possible only in an act of consciousness which destroys all the structures of the
world which might *reject* the magical and reduce
the event to its proper proportions. For example,

the window as *"object which must first be broken,"* the ten yards as *"distance which must first be covered,"* must be annihilated. This does not at all mean that consciousness in its terror *brings* the face *closer* in the sense that it *would reduce* the distance from the face to my body. To reduce the distance is still to reckon with the distance. Likewise, as long as the frightened subject can think that "the window can be broken easily, it can be opened from the outside," he is only giving rational interpretations which he proposes out of fear. In reality, the window and the distance are perceived *"at the same time"* in the act by which consciousness perceives the face behind the window. But in the very act of perceiving it they are relieved of their character of necessary *instruments*. They are perceived otherwise. The distance is no longer perceived as distance, because it is no longer perceived as "that which must first be travelled." It is perceived as the unitary *basis* of the horrible. The window is no longer perceived as *"that which must first be opened."* It is perceived as the *frame* of the horrible face. And in a general way regions are set up around me *on the basis of which* the horrible manifests itself. For the horrible *is not possible* in the deterministic world of instruments. The horrible can appear only in the kind of world whose existants are magical by nature and whose possible recourse against the existants are magical. This is rather well shown in the universe of the dream where doors, locks, walls, and arms are not recourses against the menaces of the thief or the wild animal because they are perceived in a unitary act of horror. And as the act which disarms them is the same as the one which creates them, we see the murderers cross these walls and doors. In vain do we press the trigger of our revolver—the shot does not go off. In short, to perceive any object whatsoever as horrible is to perceive it on the basis of a world which reveals itself as *already* being horrible.

Thus, consciousness can "be-in-the-World" in two different ways. The world can appear to it as a complex of instruments so organized that if one wished to produce a determined effect it would be necessary to act upon the determined elements of the complex. In this case, each instrument refers to other instruments and to the totality of instruments; there is no absolute action or radical change that one can immediately introduce into this world. It is necessary to modify a particular instrument and this by means of another instrument which refers to other instruments and so on to infinity. But the world can also appear to it as a non-instrumental totality, that is, modifiable by large masses and without an intermediary. In this case, the categories of the world will act upon consciousness immediately. They are present to it *without distance* (for example, the face which frightens us through the window acts upon us *without instruments*; there is no need for the *window* to open, for a man to leap into the *room* and walk upon the *floor*). And, reciprocally, consciousness aims at combating these dangers or modifying those objects without distance and without instruments by absolute and massive modifications of the world. This aspect of the world is entirely coherent; it is the *magical* world. We shall call emotion an abrupt drop of consciousness into the magical. Or, if one prefers, there is emotion when the world of instruments abruptly vanishes and the magical world appears in its place. Therefore, it is not necessary to see emotion as a passive disorder of the organism and the mind which comes *from the outside* to disturb the psychic life. On the contrary, it is the return of consciousness to the magical attitude, one of the great attitudes which are essential to it, with appearance of the correlative world, the magical world. Emotion is not an accident. It is a mode of existence of consciousness, one of the ways in which it *understands* (in the Heideggerian sense of "Verstehen") its "being-in-the-world."

A reflective consciousness can always direct itself upon emotion. In this case emotion appears as a structure of consciousness. It is not pure and inexpressible quality as is brick-red or the pure impression of grief—as it ought to be according to James's theory. It has a meaning; it *signifies something for my psychic life.* The purifying reflection of the phenomenological reduction can perceive the emotion insofar as it constitutes the world in a magical form. "I find it hateful *because* I am angry."

But this reflection is rare and necessitates special motivations. Ordinarily, we direct upon the emotive consciousness an accessory reflection which certainly perceives consciousness as consciousness, but insofar as it is motivated by the object: "I am angry *because* it is hateful." It is on the basis of this reflection that the passion will constitute itself.

CONCLUSION

THE PURPOSE of the theory of emotion which we have just outlined is to serve as an experiment for the establishment of a phenomenological psychology. Of course, since it is an *example*, we are prevented from giving it the development which it requires.[1] On the other hand, since it was necessary to make a clear sweep of ordinary psychological theories of emotion, we moved gradually from the psychological considerations of James to the idea of signification. A phenomenological psychology which was sure of itself and which had first set up a fresh area would begin at the very start by fixing in an eidetic image, the essence of the psychological fact which it was investigating. This is what we have tried to do for the *mental image* in a work which will soon appear. But despite these reservations of detail we hope that we have man-

[1] We should very much like our suggestions to stimulate the writing, from this point of view, of complete monographs on joy, sadness etc. We have here furnished only the schematic directions for such monographs.

aged to show that a psychic fact like emotion, which is usually held to be a lawless disorder, has a proper signification and cannot be grasped in itself without the understanding of this signification. At present we should like to mark the limits of this psychological research.

We have said in our introduction that the signification of a fact of consciousness comes down to this: that it always indicates the total human-reality which *becomes* moved, attentive, perceiving, willing, etc. The study of emotions has quite verified this principle: an emotion refers back to what it signifies. And, in effect, what it signifies is the totality of the relationships of the human reality to the world. The passage to emotion is a total modification of "being-in-the-world" according to the very particular laws of magic. But at once we see the limits of such a description; the psychological theory of emotion supposes a preliminary description of affectivity insofar as the latter constitutes the being of the human reality; that is, insofar as it is constitutive for *our* human-reality of being affective human-reality. In this case, instead of starting from a study of the emotion or the inclinations which might indicate a human reality not yet elucidated as the ultimate term of all research, an ideal term, moreover, and in all likelihood, beyond the reach of anyone who begins with the empirical, the description of affect would take place *on the basis* of the human reality described and fixed by an *a priori* intuition. The various disciplines of phenomenological psychology are *regressive*, and yet the term of their regression is *for them* a pure ideal. Those of pure phenomenology are, on the contrary, progressive. It will doubtless be asked why it is expedient in these conditions to use these two disciplines simultaneously. It seems that pure phenomenology would be sufficient. But if phenomenology can prove that emotion is in essence a realization of human-reality insofar as it is *affection*, it will be impossible for it to show that human-reality must necessarily manifest itself in *such* emotions. That there are such and such emotions, and only these, manifests without any doubt the *factitiousness* of human existence. It is this factitiousness which makes necessary a regular recourse to the empirical; it is this which, in all likelihood, will prevent psychological regression and phenomenological progression from ever coming together.